CLB 852
© 1986 Illustrations: Colour Library Books Ltd.,
    Guildford, Surrey, England.
Text filmsetting by Acesetters Ltd., Richmond, Surrey, England.
All rights reserved.
1986 edition published by Crescent Books, distributed by Crown Publishers, Inc.
Printed in Spain.
ISBN 0 517 47813 7
h g f e d c b a
Dep. Leg. B-4.670-86

# LIVING
# GHOST TOWNS

CRESCENT BOOKS
NEW YORK

If you were ever to meet a real ghost on the streets of an American ghost town, you'd be lucky if it were the shade of one Horace Austin Warner Tabor. He'd be easy to spot in any crowd of ghosts. In life he had a body like a fire hydrant with a head much too large for it, a handicap he made worse with an unusually heavy handlebar moustache. His walk alone would make him recognizable. He always looked like he was on the verge of running away, though his movements were actually quite slow. His mind seemed slow, too. In his early life no one asked him a question unless they had a lot of time to wait around for an answer. Later in his life a lot of people felt it was well worth the wait because this man was one of the most important people in the West's great Bonanza days.

They called him "Haw," which had more to do with the initials of his long string of first names than his sense of humor, which many of his contemporaries said was nonexistent. But if Haw Tabor was slow of speech and slow of wit, his career as a businessman and politician, his role in bringing culture to the Wild West, even his sex life, make him one of the most fascinating ghosts the West has ever produced.

Like so many of the larger than life characters of the American West, Tabor's roots were in the East. He was born in Vermont, learned his trade as a stonecutter in Massachusetts and met the girl he married in Maine.

Of all the human qualities that tamed the West, the ones traditional to New England were probably the most important, and Haw Tabor's bride, Augusta, seems to have had all those qualities rolled into one person. She had stamina and courage, a strong sense of loyalty, a deep religious sense and a stoicism that helped her endure the worst that man and nature could send her way. Both sent what seems to have been more than her share.

Nobody knows for sure what posessed Tabor to strike out for the West within days of his marriage in 1857. There was a depression raging in the East, but Haw had married the boss's daughter and wasn't out of work. On the other hand, working for his father-in-law possibly went against his spirit of Yankee independence. Whatever reason he gave her, Augusta didn't waste any time packing and two weeks later they were in Kansas City at the beginning of a great adventure.

By the time they claimed an abandoned homestead on the Kansas prairie, Augusta was pregnant. It didn't stop her from working the fields, of course. But by harvest time all the Tabors had to show for their first summer in the West was another mouth to feed.

Their second summer in Kansas produced more in the way of crops, but they couldn't find a way to sell any. Augusta herself provided all the cash the family had by taking in boarders.

A combination of pride and desperation prompted Haw to try his luck at digging for gold in the Pike's Peak area of Colorado rather than planting crops during the third summer. Though he had planned to send Augusta back to her father for a couple of months, she convinced him that they could take their two boarders along and live off the money they paid.

Previous pages and facing page: original buildings in the once tough and lawless mining community of Bodie, California, stand arrested in semi-decay. Above: roughly-patched shop window, and (overleaf) a worked-out mine, Bodie.

Tabor scratched for gold at Idaho Springs, west of Denver, but like so many before him he discovered that if there was gold in "them thar hills," looking for it was uncommonly hard work and finding it incredibly good luck. While Haw

worked, so did Augusta. They had taken a couple of cows with them and she made a fair amount of money selling milk. She also opened a bakery and built a reputation as a nurse, tending fevers and gunshot wounds for grateful prospectors.

Gold-mining, and all the harsh, colorful life that accompanied it, reached a climax in Bodie (these pages) in 1859.

Her patients had told her tales of Rocky Mountain winters and, when the snow began to fly, she convinced her husband that they should move to Denver. Though he hadn't found a dime's worth of gold, she had earned enough with her little enterprise to keep the family going for the winter in a furnished room. But it wasn't good enough for Haw Tabor. Leaving his wife and son behind, he went back into the snow-covered mountains to work his mine, only to find his claim had been jumped by another prospector.

The story should have ended there. But nobody who went to Colorado in the late 1850s knew the meaning of the word "discouraged." Before the winter was over, the Tabor family, boarders in tow, were on their way south and west in the general direction of Pike's Peak.

Though they dug in a lot of places along the way, the trail eventually led to California Gulch, where a man named Abe Lee had recently found what he said was "the whole state of California in a single pan." The Tabor party was among the first to follow on his heels.

Though Haw found some $5,000 worth of gold in the summer of 1859, his practical turn of mind prompted him to spend some of the time building a log cabin big enough for Augusta and their son as well as the boarders. Thanks to Augusta's equally practical turn of mind, he also made room for more boarders, and before the year was over he had expanded it to include a post office and a general store.

The place was called Boughtown in those days, probably because most of its buildings were simple shelters made of pine boughs. Tabor's cabin was the most impressive building in town until a church was built. Both had more than ten thousand potential customers to serve before the summer was over. By then they had given their town the more alluring name of Oro City.

The city shut down in the winter when it was nearly impossible to pull gold out of the frozen ground. But in the months it was operating full-tilt, Oro City was the stuff of legends. Though ordinary miners working for other people, and the majority of the population earned only $6 a day, there were fortunes to be made. The richest among them were hauling some $10,000 a day out of the ground. And for every dollar it seemed there was a gambler, a speculator, an outlaw waiting to take it off their hands. One of the more popular prostitutes claimed she made $100,000 in a single season.

Haw Tabor made a fair amount indulging his passion for poker, but his real hope was in a mine he had staked out in the hills above town. Though he obviously wasn't afraid of hard work, he had picked a spot where a rushing stream took some of the effort out of digging. It also took most of the gold away into areas claimed by other miners. The point became moot very quickly, though. Many millions in gold had been taken out of California Gulch in a few months and then suddenly it all ended. When summer came, the fortune hunters pushed on over the Continental Divide looking for new treasure and the Tabors were left with a post office that had no mail and a general store that had no customers. Oro City had become a ghost town.

Like everyone else, the Tabors decided to move on. They went to another Bonanza town called Buckskin Joe. But by that point Haw seems to have given up the idea of making a fortune in gold in favor of making a living as a storekeeper. When the gold stopped coming and the fortune hunters once again moved on, he moved his family back to Oro City, where he reopened his store and post office to serve the 50-

odd die-hard miners working almost profitless claims. Augusta continued in the boarding house business and Haw seemed content to spend the rest of his life as a small-town businessman with not much more excitement than an occasional friendly game of poker.

The real excitement was yet to come. And Haw Tabor would be at the center of it.

Though there was no gold to speak of left in California Gulch and Oro City was essentially a ghost town, it was not completely dead. There were still overlooked patches of gold and a fair amount of quartz, as well as enough lead to make digging worthwhile if not the source of fabulous riches.

Among the men willing to do the work was an old miner named "Uncle Billy" Stevens and his partner A.B. Wood. A metallurgist, Wood was fascinated by what else might be under the California Gulch hillsides. His scientific curiosity led him to discover a rich vein of silver running close to the surface.

Neither he nor Uncle Billy told anyone what they had found until after they had established a dozen claims up and down the gulch. Even when they talked about it, nobody much listened. Gold was what most people were after. But when Wood sold his claims to Marshall Field of Chicago for $40,000 a few old sourdoughs began to sit up and take notice. Within a few months, Oro City wasn't a ghost town any more. In fact, it had merged with a nameless nearby mining camp and had its name changed once again. It would forever after be known as Leadville. Its first mayor, by popular acclaim of the 300 residents, was the postmaster/storekeeper Horace Austin Warner Tabor.

By the time of the merger, Augusta's little boarding house had turned into a four-room hotel and the store had grown to include a popular barroom. Haw himself, now 50 years old, had perfected his poker game well enough to protect his enterprise from the most rapacious of gamblers and a table in his store had become yet another profit center.

As a pillar of the community with a reputation as an honest man, Tabor quickly became the depository of choice for miners who preferred not to take their valuables with them into the hills. As a storekeeper, he was also in a position to provide "grubstakes" for down-and-out miners on their way back to the wilds for one more shot at fortune. In return for the former, Tabor stood to keep everything that was left with him by miners who didn't come back alive, as often happened. In the case of the latter, grubstakes were worth a third of any riches a prospector happened to find. It was a gamble either way, but so was mining and Haw Tabor had had enough of that in his lifetime.

The now silent town of Bodie (facing page and overleaf) boasted, during its heyday, a population of about 10,000 and some 67 raucous saloons.

In the spring of 1878, one of Tabor's grubstakes changed not only his life but the history of Leadville. And there are those who say that if Haw had been watching his clients as carefully as he should have, none of it would have happened.

August Rische and George Hook had gone west to follow their trade as shoemakers and after several years of trying had wound up convinced that there was no place in the Wild West for makers of boots and shoes. They decided to try their hand at mining, but worse than knowing nothing about it, they didn't have the price of the food and tools they'd need to work a claim. It was clear they had nothing to lose, so clear in fact that no one would stake them. No one, that is, except Haw Tabor, and even he had his doubts.

Almost as much to get rid of them as anything else, Tabor finally agreed to let them have a grubstake, telling them to take what they needed, sign for it and get out. In the process, when he wasn't looking, they added a jug of whiskey to their selection and then quietly headed for the hills.

Every prospector in the history of the West has had his own system for finding paydirt. Many were unscientific about it, to be sure, but there is no recorded instance of any claim ever staked as casually as the one established by Rische and Hook. They simply walked out of town until they got tired of

In the 1880s, Leadville (above left, above and facing page), Colorado, was one of the world's greatest silver camps. Many early buildings have been preserved, including the Elks and the Tabor opera houses, and the Old Pioneer Bar. Top: Cripple Creek.

walking, a little less than a mile. They vaguely thought a hillside would be the most likely place to work and they selected one with shady trees so the work wouldn't be too hot. They dug and they sipped whiskey and they dug some more. They kept tugging at the whiskey jug until it was

empty and kept digging until they had made a hole 25 feet deep. It was enough to uncover a vein of pure silver. According to a Government survey, they had found the only spot in the whole area where the ore was that close to the surface. If they had dug even a few feet further away they might have missed it completely and gone back to shoemaking.

The mine, which they called The Little Pittsburgh, was producing more than $20,000 worth of silver a week by the time Haw Tabor sold his store and became a silver entrepreneur. His $60 investment in a grubstake for Rische and Hook earned him $2 million in less than a year without so much as getting his hands dirty.

Tabor was at the center of the bonanza that followed, buying and selling interests in mines all over the Leadville area. Though many tried, few succeeded in swindling him and in a very short time he was the richest man in a territory that was producing more than 300 tons of silver a year. More than riches, he also acquired power. He was elected lieutenant-governor of Colorado and rewarded his wife, Augusta, with

Above and facing page: the roofs of Leadville, spread below the peaks of the Rocky Mountains. Some mining and smelting continues here, though farming, ranching, and the tourist industry are now the town's mainstays.

an ornate mansion in Denver as well as a fine house in Leadville that not only had no room for boarders, but included servants who would make Mrs. Tabor's life one of ease.

She chose to spend most of her time at the Leadville house, but from the day she moved in, she became something of a recluse and little was seen of her again.

That was most assuredly not the case with her husband, who began to blossom as the decade of the 70s came to an end and loomed larger than life in the almost unbelievable 1880s.

The great silver strike took place in 1878. By the following summer Leadville was a boom town. People came from all over the country as well as from a fair number of foreign

countries and, of course, not all of them went to dig for silver. Though there were gamblers and prostitutes, pickpockets and highwaymen, there were also schoolteachers and engineers, lumberjacks and smelter workers, carpenters, blacksmiths, lawyers and doctors. There were even a few shoemakers following in the footsteps of Rische and Hook.

Like any other growing city, Leadville also attracted its share of preachers and temperance lecturers. One inspired a group of local ladies to form what they called a "praying orchestra," a forerunner of the Salvation Army. To the delight of practically no one, they cruised the streets of Leadville every evening going from saloon to saloon "offering prayer and song for the surrounding sinners." They agreed among themselves to stay in each resort until forcibly removed. History mercifully doesn't record the length of their average stay, nor is there much in the record about their impact on all those sinners. But one local newspaper pointed out that on a typical Leadville evening "it was nip and tuck between a temperance orator in one room and a gambler in the next to determine which could yell the loudest and attract the biggest crowd."

Leadville's biggest after-dark crowds were to be found on State Street, a stretch of dance halls, theaters, gambling houses, houses of prostitution, beer halls and fancy saloons. There were seven theaters in the half-mile strip, each of which had its own brass band out front each evening as soon as the sun went down. Each tried to play louder than the next and even when they played in tune, no two bands ever played the same song at the same time. After about an hour, as if by signal, the bands began a march that would take them all over town. If their fancy uniforms didn't identify their individual theatrical employers, they were followed by small boys carrying banners bigger than themselves describing the can-can dancers, "female bathers" and other attractions on the boards that night. Other small boys marched alongside the bands carrying torches so the performers could read the music. But on State Street, at least, their lamps were redundant. Not one of the buildings there wasn't without a collection of flickering kerosene torches that attracted attention while turning night into day.

These pages: fine, 19th-century interiors, Leadville.

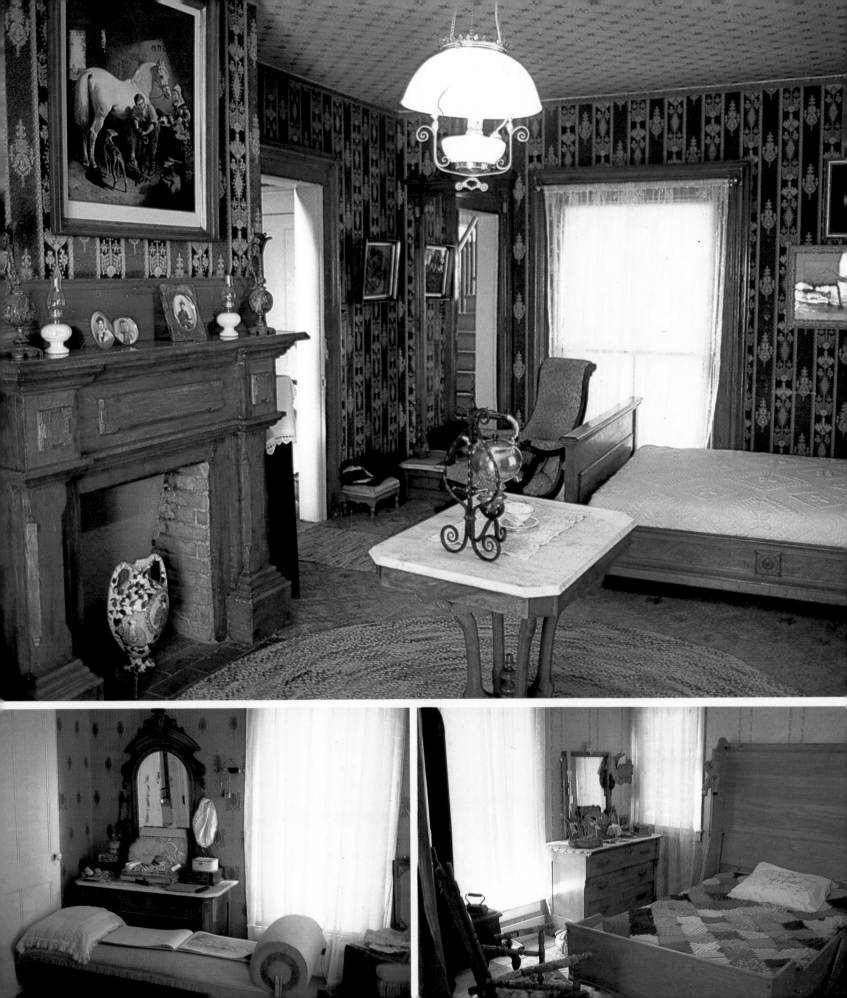

The seven nightly processions ended as they began on State Street, when the bands filed into the theaters for the evening performance, which traditionally began at nine and continued until the audience decided it was time to go home, which was never before three in the morning and usually much later. It was in the owners' best interest to keep the theaters going as late as possible. Instead of a regular admission charge, they required that the audience must patronize their bars. To put them in a drinking frame of mind and to make sure they kept at it, it was a management custom to require the young ladies appearing in the show to mingle with the customers, encouraging them to drink themselves and to buy cocktails for the cast. The cost of a cocktail was seventy-five cents, and anyone whose glass was empty for too long had the dubious pleasure of meeting one of the theater's bouncers.

There were exceptions to the custom, of course. The first and most important one was "the largest amd most elegantly appointed theater west of Chicago," the Grand Central. It regularly offered entertainments "directly from New York" at box office prices ranging from a quarter to a dollar. In 1879, the Grand Central outdid even itself with a production of "Nana, the Lovely Blonde, or, The Miser's Pet," based, it was claimed, on the novel by Emile Zola. Mr. Zola was thousands of miles away in France at the time and missed the socko ending: "A Quadrille D'Amour, in which Nana and her friends will illustrate The Poetry of Motion a la mode." It was the climax of a four-hour program that began with "Song, Dance and Mirth and Emotional Novelties; a Host of Talented Artists and *Beautiful Women!*". The handbill advertising it added that it would be a "voluptuous feast without coarseness."

There was probably enough coarseness in Leadville already, most people thought. Those who had arrived early in the boom had set up housekeeping anywhere they could find an empty space, but it wasn't long before they came up against people who insisted they should pay for that space. Even those who paid up weren't safe from possible eviction. A mining combine had acquired mineral rights to most of the land under the town and parlayed that into new profits by claiming that their rights extended to the land itself. Lots were increasing in value from as little as $10 to as much as $5,000 overnight and rents were "higher than New York City."

A prospector coming home at night might look forward to finding his house gone and his belongings tossed into the gutter if he hadn't paid what the company asked. If he was

Left: the low, green hills and the sudden rise of the Rockies outside Leadville.

unlucky enough to be at home when the eviction committee arrived, he could probably count on a few bumps on the head into the bargain.

Though mineral claims traditionally don't extend to the surface, no one had the resources to challenge this one. No one, that is, except Haw Tabor, who bought a downtown tract from them and formed the Leadville Improvement Company. He moved squatters in a more civilized fashion, added wide streets and began selling building lots at a very nice price. Coincidentally, he was also the owner of not one but two lumber companies and had the market cornered on more than a million feet of lumber being bought for Leadville buildings each and every week.

Leadville (these pages) grew, erratically, from a gold-miner's camp in 1860 to a city of about 40,000 souls by 1880. Many of the early, ornate buildings then built are carefully preserved and still in use.

But when he built an important building for himself, Tabor wisely built it of brick. What made the building important and worthy of its location at the center of the town was that it was a bank. It wasn't the only bank in town, just the most important. Tabor was suffering from the same problem as the owners of the other banks, though. They were running out of space to store all their money bags. His solution was a three-story brick building with fancy woodwork inside leading up to painted ceilings. On top he placed a metal disc representing a silver coin that glinted in the sun and could be seen in every part of town. If there was anyone who didn't know him up to that point, they knew where to find him now. And thanks to his flair for advertising, he earned a new nickname: "Silver Dollar Tabor."

Though he had owned the first hotel in town, it was a business that didn't seem to appeal to Tabor any longer. Certainly not because it wasn't a way to make plenty of money. Every day people were arriving in town and most spent their first hours there in the saloons getting the lay of the land. As evening approached, they began looking for a place to lay their head and the pickings in most cases were slim. There were a half-dozen hotels and dozens of rooming houses. But by and large most were always filled. In fact, it wasn't unusual to pack as many as ten people, each paying $1 a night, into a room with one bed. Some enterprising bonifaces put up big tents filled with beds stacked three-high which were rented in eight-hour shifts around the clock at fifty cents a shift.

But every night there were hundreds who couldn't find a place to sleep at any price. They were required to spend the night in one of the town's 120 saloons or out in the street, where the risk was quite strong that it might be their last night on earth. To spend the night on the barroom floor cost anywhere from a dime to fifty cents, depending on how close to the stove one wanted to be.

Once a newcomer decided to stay, he usually found accomodations in packing cases, holes in the ground, stables or haylofts while he was waiting to strike it rich enough to afford something better. Many didn't live long enough. If they didn't kill each other, they often fell victim to pneumonia and other diseases. The death rate was one of Leadville's best-kept secrets, rarely noticed lest it should slow the flood of new residents who could be counted on to bring money. One who did notice was Haw Tabor, who organized the Leadville Life Insurance Company.

If anyone had the impression that life was cheap in Leadville, they hadn't met up with young Maxcy Tabor, a real chip off the old block, who, as its president, kept the insurance company profitable for his father. Maxcy was also president of one of the three fire companies that were formed in the face of a constant threat that the whole city might burn down. It may explain why his father also incorporated the Leadville Fire Insurance Company. Maxcy's band of firefighters were much happier strutting around town in their snappy uniforms and distinctive straw hats than fighting fires, though. To help them out, his father the mayor issued a proclamation that every citizen of Leadville had a responsibility to respond to every fire alarm (and fight the fire with water supplied by the Leadville Water Company, another Tabor enterprise). The edict prompted many citizens to complain that every fire alarm was an open invitation to thieves to come take what they wanted while honest people were out dealing with the flames.

Tabor never got around to issuing theft insurance, probably

as $2. The same man, who could tell by the bumps "whether you are long-lived or not," also had a sideline that could make life easier to get through. He sold a patented remedy for "loss of memory, lassitude, nocturnal emissions, noises in the head, dimness of vision and aversion to society."

For diversion, members of Leadville society had a bicycle club and a roller skating club. They had a racetrack ("the best west of the Mississippi") that was home to the Leadville Trotting and Running Association. The ladies could have fancy dresses made for them by a woman who had migrated from Paris to cater to their whims and there were plenty of *Soirees Dansants*, and fancy balls to give them a genuine need for something other than store-bought gingham.

Previous pages: the former copper-mining town of Encampment, Wyoming. These pages: Central City, which sprang up on its steep, rocky hillside following Colorado's first important discovery of gold in 1859.

because as mayor he realized it was a bad risk. He had organized an eight-man police force, each with a salary of $100 a month. But he was never able to institute a program of taxation that would bring enough into the city treasury to pay their salaries. If that wasn't demoralizing enough, there was just so much eight men could do, and the citizens of Leadville, even if they did neglect to pay their taxes, had good reason to worry.

But there was plenty to take their mind off such problems, and though there was lawlessness in the streets and pestilence lurking in the alleys in the form of uncollected garbage, the average citizen of Leadville in 1880 would tell you that life there was pretty close to perfect.

They could get their hair cut by a lady barber who had come all the way from Chicago, and they could have the bumps on their head analyzed by a practicing phrenologist for as little

In the winter of 1879, Leadville was the scene of what was later remembered as the most elegant and certainly the largest party in the history of the American West. It was the Fireman's Christmas Ball held at the Central Fire House, where the dancing never stopped until the sun came up and its light was reflected in the largest collection of fancy jewels ever seen in Leadville.

But the fire companies weren't the only social institutions in this place, as was often the case in lesser American cities. Leadville even had a club called the Monroe Supporters, whose members were all blacks, even though blacks, along with Indians, were the only ethnic group considered not

These pages: the people of Central City relive the rowdy, colorful past of the town's bar-rooms and saloons. Overleaf: derelict mine, Central City.

welcome there. The Knights of Pythias had a Leadville lodge as did the Masons, the Odd Fellows, the Ancient Order of Hibernians and B'nai B'rith. There was a Y.M.C.A. as well and clubs for both Republicans and Democrats, not to mention the Elephant Club, whose members were pledged not to vote in any election whatsoever.

There were social clubs restricted to men and others dedicated to uplifting the minds and spirits of the ladies. There was a Literary Society whose members attended lectures and compared notes on books they had read. Their favorite authors were Alexandre Dumas and Jules Verne. Charles Dickens and the Bronte sisters were considered definitely *outre,* as were Thackeray and just about every other contemporary English novelist.

The city also had a plethora of temperance societies, all of which tilted at the windmills of demon rum with unbelievable passion. It all went for naught, of course. Their only solace was in the fact that although their machinations couldn't stop the building of three breweries in town, the introduction of beer cut the consumption of hard liquor somewhat.

The introduction of beer also brought beer halls, which in turn brought a new kind of society to Leadville. A beer hall tradition in the America of a century ago was the singing of songs, the old songs that many a miner had learned at his mother's knee. As the evening wore on, the mood went from beery to teary and a few bars of "Silver Threads Among the Gold" could easily reduce a burly teamster to a sentimental mess. Such are the charms of music. But what Leadville didn't have to charm its populace was an opera house. It was all that separated them from the sophistication of a New York, a Chicago or a San Francisco. The man best able to remedy that, of course, was Horace Austin Warner Tabor, the culture-hungry transplant from the sophisticated Northeast.

Always one to cover his bets, Tabor incorporated on office building into the elegant brick structure that housed his new opera house. He connected it with an overhead bridge to a hotel next door and leased its owner's space for a few extra guest rooms. The ground floor was a saloon, with a few poker tables to hold patrons who might find the on-stage drama less than entertaining.

These pages: a healthy tourist industry, based on Central City's mining and architectural heritage, now provides a major part of the town's income.

The theater itself was modestly called "the finest west of the Mississippi," and it may well have been. Tabor's own description said: "All the appointments are first-class in every respect in this temple of amusement. The scenery is artistic and under the full flood of gaslight (Tabor owned the gas company, by the way) it is the cosiest place for lovers of the legitimate drama to throw off the cares of life and yield to the fascinations of music and imagery."

Though it was called an opera house, the nightly fare ran more to melodramas than to grand opera. Shakespearean plays were popular, too, even though the Great Books fans had chosen to shun English writers. Grand opera arrived there in the theater's third season.

The perpetrator was an Englishwoman named Emma Abbott, whose arrival in town was indeed a social event of huge proportions. The local newspaper reported that many of the men in the audience had not only taken their pants out of their boots for the first time in memory, but some had actually taken the time to polish the boots. Miss Abbott had done a little polishing of the librettos of the operas she presented, which included La Traviata. She had a fixation that most opera plots were immoral and much too full of passionate love, and she took it on herself to rewrite them, censoring what she considered unacceptable. In some cases she added music as well. One opera in her repertoire featured a chorus of "Swannee River," another included "Nearer My God To Thee."

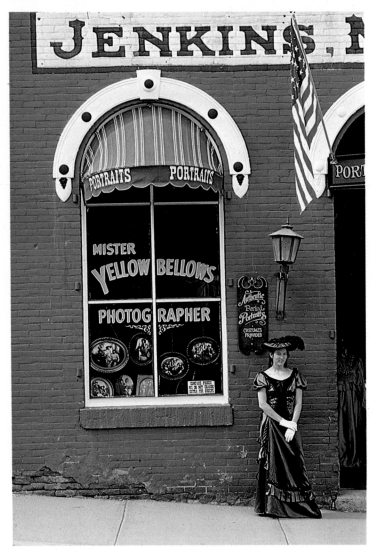

These pages: Central City's Victorian-style shop fronts. Overleaf: gold-mining continues at Central City, combining old and modern methods.

Though her concern for Leadville's morals must have impressed some of the people, most agreed that grand opera, at least as interpreted by Miss Abbott, was better left to the swells in Chicago or New York.

But there were other diversions to be indulged in at the Tabor Opera House. One of the most memorable was a lecture by the endlessly fascinating Oscar Wilde, who had come as much to satisfy his own curiosity as to enlighten the

ruffians of the Wild West on the lofty topics of art and culture. The people of Leadville were as curious about him as he was about them, and he wasn't without a little crowd of gawkers from the moment he got off the train.

In the 1860s, Central City (these pages) vied with Denver in importance. Then, the town's population approached 15,000; today, it stands at a few hundred.

Though his American tour had been marked by hostile demonstrations of disdain for his rather unorthodox outlook on life, there were no such insults waiting for him in Leadville. Possibly they were speechless, possibly they were disarmed when Haw Tabor took the lecturer down into a silver mine, where a dozen miners were waiting for him with jugs of whiskey. It was one of the hard and fast rules of the West that when a whiskey jug was passed it was insulting to its owner not to take a swig from it. In this case there were a dozen jugs to be passed, and by the time the ritual was over, Wilde was the only one in the party with all of his senses intact.

His lecture at the Opera House had everyone's head swimming. Its title was "The Practical Application of the Aesthetic Theory to Exterior and Interior House Decoration, With Observations on Dress and Personal Ornament."

After the show it was his turn to be enlightened, and the place chosen by his hosts for a night on the town was the biggest and undisputedly most popular saloon in Leadville,

Pop Wyman's. Wyman's place had everything a man could want, from a gambling casino to a dance hall to a theater and special rooms for "private entertainments." Though he was proud of the fact that the girls in his place were the prettiest in all of Colorado and was pleased to give them an opportunity to make quite a bit more than the ten dollars a week he paid them, Pop Wyman had brought a touch of the Puritan with him from back East. He didn't allow married men in his gambling casino, nor anyone drunk at his bar. He didn't allow foul language and encouraged his customers to take a little time to browse through a Bible he kept on a wooden stand just inside the door. His was the establishment that featured a sign famous throughout the West: "Don't Shoot The Piano Player." Though many may have been tempted to break this and most of Wyman's other rules from time to time, he had his own private police force on the premises to make sure they didn't.

Pop Wyman wasn't the only one in Leadville with a personal constabulary. Most of the rich mine owners had them, but none had an army as impressive as Haw Tabor's Highland Guards. His 64-man bodyguard was outfitted in livery that would have been the envy of Bonnie Prince Charlie. Their Scottish bonnets had white plumes and silver buckles. They wore kilts in a royal Stuart plaid and carried daggers in their long red stockings.

Tabor's guards impressed everybody in Leadville except, of course, the thieves and murderers who were beginning to make life unpleasant, to say the least. His response was to form a second small army, this time a mounted unit he called the Tabor Light Cavalry. There were fifty-five of them, dressed in fancy blue coats and shiny gold helmets. Proclaiming himself a general, Tabor personally led his men around town dressed in a gold-trimmed jacket and wearing a sword he had especially made, rumor had it, for $50.

The desperadoes winked and went on about their business.

Lawlessness seemed to have become an epidemic in Leadville. In a single month in 1880 no less than 40 people were arrested for murder. There are no figures available for the number that got away with murder in this city with its less than perfect police department.

The citizens themselves formed vigilante committees and dealt with the problem with a length of rope and a high tree. But eventually the problem grew too big even for them as a labor war broke out in the mines. Before it ended, the governor put Leadville under martial law and sent in the militia to enforce a strict set of new laws. In their first day, they arrested four hundred on charges of vagrancy. The strike was eventually broken and the crime wave subsided dramatically, but Leadville never completely recovered from the events of the summer of 1880.

There was still plenty of silver to take from the ground, but investors stopped providing the capital to make it possible. The tide of immigration all but stopped as well and the freespending "there's no tomorrow" attitude of the people already there began to change. Business fell in saloons and theaters and stores. The impact was hardest-felt in the banks, many of which failed. But in spite of what to Leadville were hard times, the town didn't die. In fact, two years later it

Silver City (facing page), in the Owyhee Mountains of Idaho, was founded in 1863 by settlers from nearby Ruby City. Above: Silver City Schoolhouse Museum.

produced more silver, $17 million worth, than any other year in its history. But by then many of the pillars of the community weren't there to see it happen. Haw Tabor was among the first to abandon Leadville, and by 1882 he was cutting quite a figure in Denver.

For his first trick, he built a six-story building ("ornate but tasteful") near the center of town. Every stone used in its construction was carried to the Rocky Mountains from Ohio. Then, before the paint was dry, he sent to Ohio for more building blocks and began work on a second structure which would also include wainscotting made from the finest cherry imported from Japan, and columns and lintels made from marble quarried in far-off Italy.

Tabor took all the credit for the architecture of both, which he said had been inspired by a recent Grand Tour back East. He had a professional architect helping him, of course. He had been sent to London and Paris for inspiration.

Each of the two buildings, as was Tabor's custom, had revenue-producing offices and retail stores, but the second had something very special indeed, the Tabor Grand Opera House. It was, as they say, something God Himself would have created if he had had the money. The three tiers of boxes were lined with pure silk fabric especially made in France and topped with canopies made by Italian artisans. It had a stained glass dome and a hand-cut crystal chandelier. It had elaborate murals throughout and the curtain, ironically, featured a massive painting of a Roman ruin, a subject apparently inspiring to the former stonecutter from Vermont who commissioned it. All in all, the Tabor Grand made his opera house in Leadville look like a high school auditorium.

The Grand Opening was a fancy dress affair and featured no less an opera company than the one headed by the infamous Miss Emma Abbott. She was better received in Denver than in Leadville and was held over for two weeks, all the while solicitously protecting the morals of the apparently more sophisticated Denverites.

The ordinary fare at the Tabor Grand ran to productions of Gilbert and Sullivan, melodramas, minstrel shows and

Almost all the 19th-century predecessors of Silver City's present inhabitants (this page) possessed a silver mine in the cellar of their homes, and a maze of tunnels ran beneath the city's streets and buildings (facing page).

culturally uplifting lectures. But it was an important stop for every major touring theatrical and musical organization and in its heyday featured the likes of Lily Langtry, Joseph Jefferson and Edwin Booth.

Haw Tabor liked having such names linked to his, but what he liked even more was making money, and it was clear he had a flair for it. His mining interests were netting him hundreds of thousands of dollars a week and he still had banks and insurance companies among other interests to fall back on should the need arise. He owned mines all over the Southwest as well as in Colorado and through one of his companies he controlled a 400 square mile piece of the country of Honduras.

But was he happy? What do you think?

What Haw Tabor really wanted was a career in politics. And as if to prove that money can indeed buy happiness, he began putting dollars where they could do the most good for him in the high councils of the Republican Party. He'd had a taste of the power of politics as mayor of Leadville and as lieutenant-governor of Colorado, but the taste only inspired an almost lustful appetite for more.

What looked like an opportunity came when one of Colorado's seats in the United States Senate was vacated. It was up to the governor to appoint someone to finish out the term and Mr. Tabor decided that there was no better choice than he. But there was a problem. In spite of his money, his business ability and even his charm, the governor didn't like Haw Tabor.

Tabor had no choice other than to take his case directly to the people. The people he convinced even marched on Denver demanding that he get the appointment, but the governor was unmoved. His next move was to appoint someone else.

The would-be senator finally got what he wanted the following year, when the Colorado legislature elected him to a thirty-day term in Washington. Not much time, but to Tabor it was better to have loved and lost than not to have loved at all.

He was much less lucky in love as it turned out.

One of the disadvantages of a life of politics is that it sometimes opens your personal life to scrutiny. Two years before he began seriously lusting after a seat in the Senate, Mr. Tabor had secretly divorced his wife. It was such a well-kept secret, in fact, even Augusta didn't know it had happened. It was legal enough, but he had obtained the divorce in a backwoods court where the judge didn't require that both parties appear. Tabor made sure that the whole thing would be kept secret by bribing a court clerk to cover up the record. It was simply done by pasting together some of the pages in the record book.

But nothing is forever, of course. Eventually a new court clerk came on the scene and in his curiosity couldn't resist finding out why those pages were pasted together. When he found out, he couldn't resist seeking out poor Augusta to tell her about it.

Needless to say, she was shocked, not to mention hurt and angry. She hauled Haw to court with the charge that he hadn't contributed to her support for two years and that she had been forced once again to take in boarders. Tabor was able to have the case thrown out, but the seeds of scandal were already planted. To pave the way for his anticipated career in politics, he was eventually forced to reopen the case and magnanimously announced that Augusta had agreed to let him give her a million-dollar property settlement. It all became official two days before he left for Washington to become a thirty-day wonder.

Augusta, never much of a public figure, almost completely dropped from sight after the divorce. Six years later she emerged briefly to sign a lease on Denver's Brown Palace Hotel, which was run for the next two years by her son Maxcey. In 1895 she died quietly, apparently never understanding exactly what happened to her marriage.

On the other hand, people in every part of the country were sure *they* knew.

As a senator, Haw Tabor made more of a name for himself in Washington society than in the halls of Congress. He found plenty of willing poker players and his expensive clothes and flashy jewelry gave Washingtonians plenty to talk about for months to come. But what they and the whole country were talking about most was an event that took place two days before his 30-day term of office ended. Haw Tabor got married again.

The wedding at the Willard Hotel was attended by no less a person than President Chester A. Arthur and other Washington notables, all of whom agreed that the bride was possibly the loveliest any of them had ever seen.

They may have been right. Even without the $90,000 diamond necklace and other jewelry the bridegroom had given her, this 22 year-old blue-eyed blonde would have made any man among them turn his head. Her name was Elizabeth McCourt, but back in Colorado she was known far and wide as "Baby Doe," the former wife of Harvey Doe, a ne'er-do-well she had shed for non-support.

Facing page: Silver City bar-room, where the atmosphere of the town's mining days is faithfully preserved. Overleaf: the Idaho Hotel, Silver City.

She didn't lack for support once she met Haw Tabor and it was rumored that he had "kept" her for some time back in Denver. If that rumor didn't have enough tongues wagging, there was more to come. Within days of the wedding, the priest who had performed the ceremony said the whole thing was illegal because it was against the rules of his church to marry divorced persons. In this case, *both* parties were divorced and he was shocked.

Silver City (these pages) grew up as a much more stable, law-abiding community than many mining camps. Facing page: scenes little changed since the town's early years.

Tabor retorted that he was just as shocked. "He never asked us if we were divorced," he indignantly told the press. The whole affair got even murkier when it was revealed that the wedding was little more than pure theater. Haw and Baby Doe, it turned out, had already been married six months earlier.

Tabor's political fortunes turned after that, but his 30-day adventure in Washington entitled him to be ever known as "Senator Tabor." Because of the scandal, he and his bride were generally ignored by Denver "society," but if either of them was offended by the slight, they didn't complain about it. They lived in a fashionable house and entertained fashionable people passing through. Baby Doe gave birth to two babies, both daughters. The first, who they always referred to as "the Golden Eagle," they named Elizabeth Bonduel Little, the second was called Rose Mary Echo Silver Dollar. Her pet name was "Silver."

Their father poured huge sums of money into unsuccessful attempts to become first governor, then senator, then governor again. And he poured even more into speculative

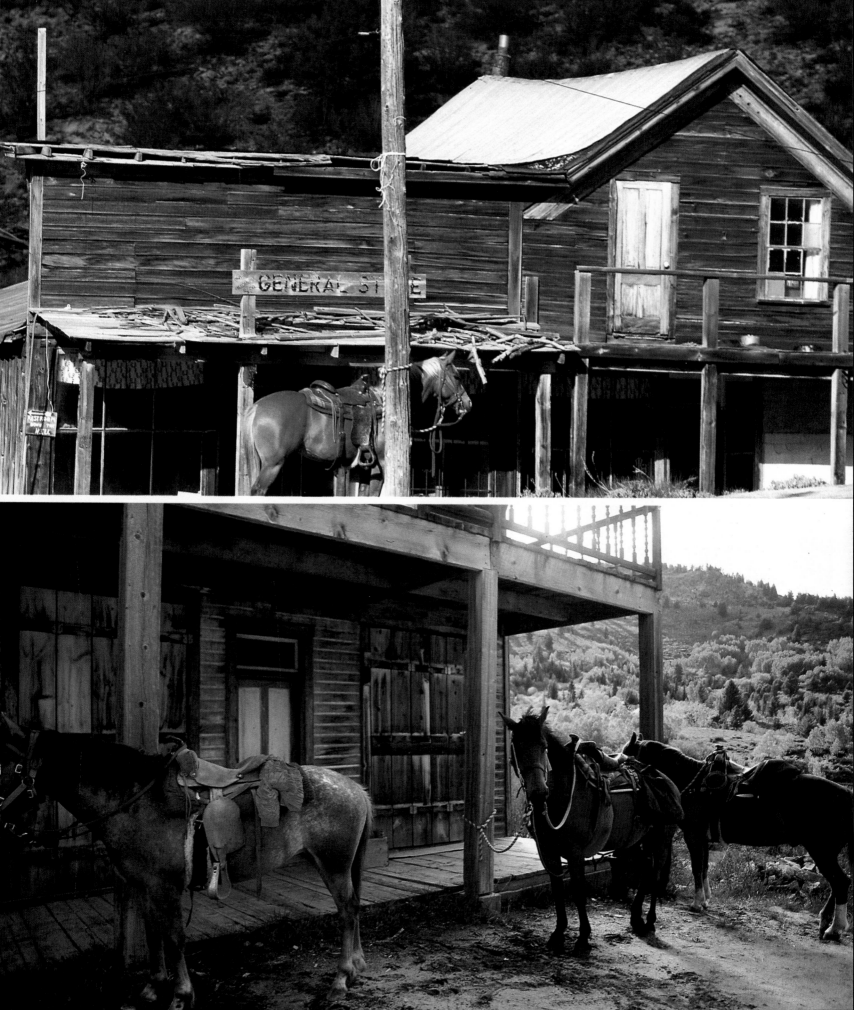

investments. Then, almost overnight, his luck turned. His investments began losing money. His mines stopped producing. Even his luck at poker apparently ran out. Nothing seemed to be going right.

Then one day the Federal Government announced that it was going to stop buying silver to make coins and Silver Dollar Tabor's fortunes took an irreversible turn for the worse. As his funds dried up, he even tried to go back to prospecting. Everything he had was sold, but nothing he was able to do produced enough cash to settle his debts, not to mention to support his wife and daughters. Finally he was able to use what little political influence he had left, ironically with the Democrats, to get a salaried job as postmaster in Denver. In another twist of irony, it was the same job he had held not many miles away when fortune began to smile at him.

Tabor died quietly a year later in the single furnished room he shared with his family. He was 70 years old. His widow was 38. His only legacy to her was a played-out mine in the hills above Leadville. He had named it "Matchless" when he bought it twenty years earlier for $117,000. Though he had profited on the investment hundreds of times over, he chose never to part with it because he was convinced it would one day be the new El Dorado.

Though her brother had been involved in some of her husband's enterprises and came away from the crash virtually unhurt, Baby Doe refused all his offers of help. Instead she packed up her teenage daughters and went back to Leadville, where they took up residence in a shack next to the Matchless shaft.

The girls didn't stay with her very long. The Golden Eagle was first to fly. She went to Chicago, where she ultimately got married and managed to vanish without a trace. Silver announced that she was going to enter a convent and nearly succeeded in vanishing herself. She died under mysterious circumstances, many said she had been murdered, in Chicago in 1925.

Their mother, meanwhile, kept up her search for the silver her husband had told her was in the matchless mine. Her single-minded determination would have put any old sourdough to shame. By day she sloshed around the mine pit wearing heavy boots and dirty overalls. By night she guarded her treasure with a shotgun on her knee, though of course no one but she believed there was actually a treasure to guard.

She kept up her unproductive search in all kinds of weather for about a month short of 37 years. Then in March, 1936, the people of Leadville noticed that there were no sounds coming from the mine and that none of them had seen her for a week or more.

They found her frozen to death on the floor of her cabin. Though 75 years old, she had kept much of the blonde beauty that had earned her the name Baby Doe. Her name was immortalized in Douglas Moore's opera *The Ballad of Baby Doe*, which in 1958 introduced Beverly Sills to the stage on the New York City Opera.

But in Leadville, Colorado, neither she nor Haw Tabor, nor Augusta Tabor for that matter, will ever be forgotten. Their ghosts still walk the streets there. You might see them over near the Opera House or up by the cabin at the Matchless. But if you don't see them, that doesn't mean they're not there. After all, what would Leadville be without them?

It's questionable whether anyone outside of Colorado would remember them without the Moore opera. Visitors to Leadville today invariably refer to the Tabor Opera House as the "Baby Doe Opera House," and they aren't always sure where they've heard the name before.

But if there is such a thing as immortality, the 19th century American who came as close as anyone to achieving it began his rise to fame in a Nevada mining town that is still one of the most famous of all the ghost towns of the West.

He grew up in a little river town in Missouri and had tried all sorts of ways to make a living before giving up on all of them and joining his brother, the Secretary of the Territory of Nevada, in Carson City during the summer of 1861.

He worked for his brother for a while before he was, as he put it, "smitten with the silver fever." He became a prospector and, if his own story is to be believed, a near millionaire. He was so close to riches, he said, his mind worked harder than his hands. "I was altering and amending the plans for my house," he wrote later, "thinking over the propriety of having the billard room in the attic, instead of on the same floor as the dining room." He also dreamed of a Grand Tour of Europe as he hacked away at the rock. "I managed to get it all laid out as to route and length of time to be devoted to it — everything with one exception — namely, whether to cross the desert from Cairo to Jerusalem per camel or to go by sea."

He eventually did have a fine house with a billiard room and he crossed the desert from Cairo to Jerusalem "per camel." But he and his partners lost their silver mine before they struck it rich and he was forced to seek refuge in a salaried job. The pay was $25 a week, "a fortune, a sinful and lavish waste of money," the job was city editor of the *Territorial Enterprise*, the daily newspaper in the boom town of Virginia City.

Much has been done to restore Virginia City (facing page), Nevada, to the appearance of its 1870s heyday.

Present-day Virginia City (these pages) thrives on the harsh romance of its past.

The young man's name was Samuel L. Clemens, but for his career as a newspaperman he shortened it to Mark Twain. Except for letters to the editor of the *Enterprise*, Clemens had never been a writer before, but he had never dug for silver before going to Nevada, either, and by comparison, a reporter's notebook was a less unwieldy tool than a hard-to-balance long-handled shovel.

Almost at the same time that he became a journalist, Virginia City became what he called the "livest" city in America. As would happen in Leadville a decade later, it swarmed with people day and night. It had the same ratio of gambling palaces and saloons, bordellos and theaters. It had the same uniformed firefighters and brass bands strutting in its streets. It had the same problems with murderers and highwaymen. For a newspaperman required to fill empty columns of space each day, it was heaven on earth.

If you don't mind climbing steep hills and don't suffer from acrophobia, Virginia City seems very close to heaven. It sits on the slopes of Mount Davidson high over the Nevada desert. Today it is reached by a modern, winding road, but in its glory days it was a major challenge just to get there. It was worth the challenge, though. In just under 80 years, more than $900 million worth of gold and silver were taken from the fabulous Comstock lode that runs under its streets.

The lode was named for Henry Comstock, a sheepherder who was known far and wide as "Old Pancake" for the mainstay of his diet, the simplest food of all to prepare. He was never a very serious prospector and, though he scratched around the hills for years, he never made a serious strike. But he was an opportunist who talked a good fight and his tongue earned him a place in the history of the West.

Gold was discovered in the Nevada hills in 1849 by a party of Mormons on their way to the rich fields of California. Over

Above: Piper's Opera House in Virginia City, Nevada, beautifully restored to its Victorian splendor.
Facing page: (top) a glittering hotel bar, and (bottom) the Bucket of Blood Saloon, Virginia City.

the next two years, dozens of would-be miners passed through the same canyons and most found gold there, but to a man they kept pushing west, where the grass was greener and the streams were tinged with yellow gold.

One of the reasons why they kept moving was that the Nevada gold was mixed with blue dirt and it was too much like work to separate it out. Few knew and even fewer cared that the blue dirt was silver. In 1856 a pair of brothers named Grosch arrived and began quietly getting rich from a mine whose location they kept a deep secret. Their secret died with them a year later, and Pancake Comstock became single-minded about uncovering it. He searched

everywhere, and though he didn't dig much he left monuments all over indentifying likely spots as his own claims.

By that point a steady stream of miners was staking other claims and finding a respectable amount of gold, but they also found that accursed blue dirt, which wound up in huge piles of waste. Finally, a Californian who was a little smarter than the rest sent some of the waste off to be assayed. The report valued the dirt as worth nearly $5,000 a ton in silver and a bit over $3,000 in gold.

These pages: mining-era buildings in Virginia City, put to good use by the tourist trade. Facing page: (top) Storey County Court House, (bottom left) Piper's Opera House, and (bottom right) the Fourth-Ward School.

From that day on the California Gold Rush ended and anyone who sincerely wanted to be rich was headed back east over the Sierras. The little tent city on the slopes of what was then called Sun Mountain was about to become a metropolis. It didn't have a name until one night in 1860 when a sourdough named "Old Virginny" staggered out of his tent for another bottle of whiskey. On his way back, he tripped and dropped the bottle. As he watched the precious liquid sink into the ground, he stared after it and mumbled, "I christen this place Virginia."

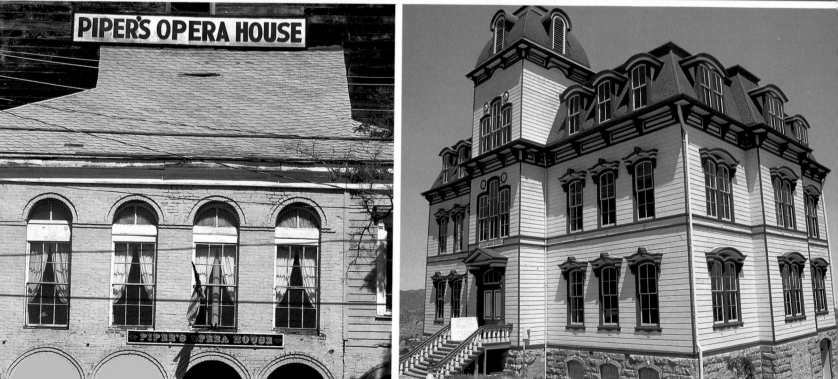

PIPER'S OPERA HOUSE

Above: miners on the steep slopes of Mogollon, New Mexico, where (below) a mule train files along the main street. Facing page: the shell of a worked-out mine, Mogollon.

Even though there were fabulous riches under it, it was probably the most unlikely place for a city in the history of the world. One stretch along the road reaching it rose 2,000 feet in five miles. The overall grade was 12 percent. The city itself was plagued with sudden windstorms called "Washoe Zephyrs" which picked up buildings and tossed them off the mountainside with frightening regularity. The fact that it almost never rained was reason enough not to put a city there, the hot sun in a cloudless sky was an even better one.

The laborers who worked the mines earned every penny of their six dollar-a-day salary. It was so oppressively hot inside the mines that the workers were continuously sprayed with water to keep them cool. Even at that, they worked just 15 minutes out of every hour, spending the rest of the time in front of huge fans whose air came to them over blocks of ice.

Work in most mines went on around the clock, as did the movement of pack trains of mules and horses bringing supplies in and treasure out. The only difference between night and day for the teamsters was that some of the nighttime pack trains were made up of camels, who couldn't be worked in daylight because the sight of them frightened

Cinco de Mayo    Mogollon N.M.

Above: Mexican miners celebrating a traditional, 5th May holiday with a parade down the main street, Mogollon. Left: a mule train. These teams, often 20 mules strong, hauled raw gold and silver ore down from the Mogollon Mountains for smelting. Facing page: Mogollon today.

the horses. They were all finally replaced by a laboriously-built railroad that connected Virginia City with Reno, 52 miles away. In its heyday, as many as 50 trains a day made the round trip.

Mark Twain, meanwhile, was doing as well, in his way, as Virginia City itself. In a matter of months his salary was raised from $25 to $40 a week and he was able to brag that he

almost never bothered to pick up the two $20 goldpieces when payday came around. He hadn't gone back to prospecting and he wasn't doing anything dishonest or illegal. But he was growing moderately rich, as was just about everybody else, just by living in Virginia City.

He said that the city and the mountainside around it had more mines than it had miners and that the overwhelming majority of them were worthless holes in the ground. But, of course, in the Virginia City of the 1860s, nothing was worthless. Not as long as there were such things as faith and hope.

The hopeful were wildcat miners who dug pits everywhere, including in the streets of the town, looking for a ledge that might extend out from the main lead that was making some men incredibly rich. Once they had a mine established, they legalized it, gave it a fancy name and had stock certificates

printed. The certificates entitled purchasers to a piece of the mine, a foot at a time. In the main Comstock lead, a foot could be worth several thousand dollars, and every wildcatter sincerely believed that once he got down to a solid shelf, his "feet" would be worth as much if not more.

If they had incredible hope and undying faith, the prospectors of the Comstock also had a liberal amount of charity, which helps explain why Mark Twain felt that

These pages: the homes and once-crowded social centers of Mogollon, now left largely to slow decay. Overleaf: Virginia City in Montana, founded in 1863.

picking up his pay would only add unnecessary weight to his pockets. The certificates were much lighter and easier to come by. If a miner liked your smile, he'd be likely to give you a fist-full of his stock. "If you are coming up the street with a couple of baskets of apples, and you meet a friend, you naturally invite him to take a few," said Mark Twain. "That describes the condition of things in Virginia in the 'flush times.'" He said that he himself had a trunk-full of stock which he sold as the need arose. He added that every man in town owned stock in fifty different mines and every man in town believed he would be fabulously rich one day soon. "Think of a city with not one solitary poor man in it!," he wrote.

If no one was poor, some were richer than others, including a young miner named George Hearst, whose fortune became the basis of the newspaper empire founded by his son, William Randolph Hearst.

At its height, the population of Virginia City reached about 15,000. By the beginning of 1865, most of them were sure that the Comstock had produced about all that it was going

to. Among them was Mark Twain, who said he was going to New York to explore its virgin territory for the sale of silver mining stock.

He got as far as San Francisco, where his intention was to go back to "the States" by boat. A newspaper report that he had been beaten to New York by other, more professional stock salesmen, prompted him to seek other ways of making a living. The rest is history.

The history of Virginia City was far from over at that point. It was nearly wiped out twice by fire, in 1863 and 1875. Naturally, it was rebuilt quickly each time. It reached the heights in 1873, when professional miners joined forces with

San Francisco financial interests to get to the "Heart of the Comstock." When they found it, their stock was worth some $160 million. It took them four years to dig out the high grade silver and gold and during that time their stock paid dividends of more than a million a month. By 1877, there were more than 750 miles of tunnels under the slopes of Mount Davidson.

By then it was a city of fine Victorian houses, with four churches, one of which had a bell cast from pure silver. The streets themselves were paved with waste from the mines laced with low-grade gold and silver. There was a saloon "every fifteen feet," and five breweries to keep them supplied. It was estimated that in 1880 alone, 75,000 gallons of hard liquor were consumed, not to mention thousands more of beer and wine. It had an opera house, of course, and many of the saloons had backroom space for patrons to bet their money on the outcome of a fight between a dog and a panther or a bear and a bull.

Most of the money that developed the mines around Virginia City came from across the border in California, and most of the profits were carried back to Nob Hill in San Francisco. It was only fitting. The people who worked the Comstock were either born in California or had gone there from back East with nothing more on their mind than getting rich.

Virginia City is still a living town, and, while some are derelict (above), over twenty of its early buildings have been restored and are open to the public. Right: Victorian-style saloon.

Established following the discovery of gold at Alder Gulch, Virginia City (these pages) grew rapidly, and served as the territorial capital of Montana between 1865 and 1875. The Capitol is among several buildings reconstructed in brick and native stone.

It hadn't always been that way. The western side of the Sierra Nevada Mountains and the rich valley of the Sacramento River were part of Mexico in the first half of the 19th century, and the men who ran it weren't too pleased when a Gringo named John Sutter asked for a land grant in the valley in 1841. But he had become a Mexican citizen and not many people in Mexico City were interested in going north anyway. They thought he was crazy, in fact. Getting across the high Sierras was an adventure that didn't interest many Americans, especially in view of the fact they had to cross a desert first. But in spite of the hardships, there was a steady stream of mountain men and Mormons in search of greener pastures, and there was probably no greener spot in the West

than Sutter's. His 76-square-mile tract was dominated by a fort surrounded by prosperous farms that served as a supply center for the pilgrims who managed the harrowing trip across the mountains. Most of those who did went north and established a substantial community of Americans in the Spanish territory. In 1846 a small American military force moved in and over the next 18 months waged an odd little war that ended with U.S. ownership of California. The treaty that made it official didn't come a moment too soon.

Exactly 22 days after the treaty was signed, James Marshall went out to inspect a new sawmill he was building for Sutter. At the edge of the stream that would drive the mill he found flakes of what appeared to be gold. It was. The very reason why the Spanish had marched north from Mexico 300 years before was to find gold and they had long-since given up. That it was there at all was bad enough. That it was found less than a month after they gave the place away must have resulted in a great deal of gnashing of teeth down in Mexico

City. But it was nothing compared to the anguish that was felt at Sutter's Fort. John Sutter had spent seven years building a utopia and it had made him a very happy man. The presence of gold, he thought, meant that his farm workers would all leave him and the land he had developed would be ruined. He was absolutely right. Sutter and Marshall tried to keep the discovery secret, but within months the fields were overrun with fortune hunters. It was said that by the middle of 1848 there wasn't a single able-bodied man left in San Francisco, Monterey or Santa Cruz. Ships in San Francisco Bay lost their entire crews. Soldiers deserted their posts and other soldiers sent to bring them back deserted too. And that was before the Gold Rush actually began.

The real invasion took place in 1849, and in less than two years the population of California went from 15,000 to 100,000. Most of them had their eye on the 120-mile strip of the Sierra foothills, where a single panful of dirt netted $1500 for one of the Forty-Niners and another dug $17,000 worth of gold in a week from a shallow, 100-foot trench.

James Marshall, the man who started it all, never managed to profit from his discovery. The site of the sawmill on the American River near Coloma was taken over by tougher men who hired armed guards to keep him away. He appealed to the courts, but by then the trespassers had gotten so rich they were able to buy "justice" for themselves. Native Californians who had not been able to stake profitable claims fast enough despised him for what he had done to their state and hounded him into leaving. He eventually went back to California where he died a pauper.

One of the places he searched for new riches was near the town of Deer Creek Diggings, a place that had been a gathering point for hunters and trappers back in the 1830s. By the time Marshall arrived there it had been renamed "Nevada" and it was on its way to becoming the third largest city in California.

In 1850 Nevada's population had topped 12,000, most of which was miners who were pulling some $4 million worth of gold from its gravel each year. When Wells Fargo opened an office there, they changed the name to Nevada City, and it became an important destination for new arrivals in the gold fields who had chosen to make the trip on one of the six stagecoaches that went there each day.

Passengers were disgorged at the still-standing National Hotel, where they usually repaired to the bar famous all over the West for the fact that its average take was a thousand dollars a day. The drink that made it famous was Pisco punch, made, the owners claimed, with brandy imported all the way from Peru.

The Nevada City Assay Office also had two claims to fame. It had the reputation of being the only such establishment that was never held up nor robbed. It was also where the first samples of the blue dirt from Virginia City was tested and found to be so rich. The latter event nearly turned Nevada City into a ghost town in 1859 when almost everyone left to try their hand at silver mining.

But the city still exists and there are few places in California where the Gold Rush Days still seem as real after all these years.

At the other end of the Mother Lode, the little town of Hornitos brings back less gentle memories. It was a Mexican village before the Forty Niners arrived and the newcomers found entertainment there in the form of wild fandangoes and fiestas. According to one legend, two Mexican dance hall girls spent the better part of one night in the plaza stalking each other with shawls in one hand and daggers in the other. By morning, both had died from loss of blood. Another tells the tale of a Chinese miner who was imprisoned for shooting an American. The whole town was up in arms and tried to lynch him, but the stone walls and iron door of the jail protected him. Then one of the Americans offered the prisoner some tobacco. When he reached out for it through the window, the mob grabbed his hand and systematically pulled him limb from limb.

People came from all over the world to get rich in the California gold fields and most were accepted on their own terms. But no one seemed able to accept the Chinese on any terms and whenever a Chinese miner found anything that looked promising, it was almost certain that there would be a band of other miners waiting to take it away. For the most part the Chinese moved meekly on, but many got rich by reworking abandoned claims that had been given up in the face of hard work. Some who ran laundries got rich by sifting the gold dust from the water they had used to wash miners' clothes.

It's entirely possible that a Chinese man lies in the grave at Grass Valley whose tombstone reads: "Lynched by Mistake. The Joke's on Us!". It is also likely that no Chinese miner ever set foot in Bodie, a mining camp near the Nevada border.

From 1876 to 1880, Bodie was known as one of the West's toughest towns, and any rascal who drifted into any other town was usually whispered to be a "bad man from Bodie." Like every other boom town, Bodie had its share of saloons

Facing page: (top) wooden boardwalks front decorative facades in Virginia City. (Bottom) the more ramshackle side of the area.

and dance halls, boarding houses, gambling dens and ladies of the evening. Its gold mines were producing a steady half-million dollars a month and there were banks to keep it safe, including one built by San Francisco's Mark Hopkins. It had churches and it had lodge halls, but what it didn't have was a police force or a court house or a jail.

Instead it had two cemeteries. One was reserved for the law-abiding citizens; the other, much larger, was for all the rest. There were often several funerals a day in the latter, usually for victims of gunfights or overindulgence in what passed for bourbon in this desolate outpost high above the treeline.

Bodie's population was almost 20,000 in its heyday, and though no one lives there now, it attracts plenty of visitors. Because of its 10,000-foot altitude, the thin, dry air has preserved it almost perfectly as a monument to its days of glory.

But for every Bodie, there were dozens of mining camps just as important to the history of California that have vanished without so much as a memory. Places with names like Git Up and Git, Poverty Flat, Whiskey Slide, Jesus Maria, Lazy Man's Canyon, Rough and Ready and Yellow Dog were mostly destroyed by fire or simple neglect. In their day, though, most of them were the direct opposite of the image of lawlessness that was created by cities like Bodie. Most were run by simple rules doggedly obeyed by everyone. It was one of the great examples of democracy at work in a country that claims to have set the standard for the world, but sometimes forgets what it means.

One of the saddest chapters in the history of the American democracy is the country's treatment of the Indians in the West. The final elements of the story involve a general named Custer, a Sioux chief named Sitting Bull and the largest vein of gold ever discovered in the Western Hemisphere.

As the country moved west, the Indian "problem" was usually handled in combat, with the red men the ultimate losers. In the process, their hunting grounds were moved many times and reduced with each successive move. Finally, the "Great White Father" settled the whole thing by giving them the territory around the Black Hills of South Dakota. "This is it," said the makers of the treaty. The Indians were told they could stay there unmolested forever and never have to fight, or move, again.

The weary Indians were satisfied. The hills were covered with trees, it was where the Thunder God made his home, buffalo were plentiful and the land itself was hostile to the white man.

Unfortunately, years before, a Sioux chief had boasted to a missionary that there was gold in the Black Hills. He never said where, and the incident was forgotten. By the early 1870s, though, most of the known gold fields in the West were generally played out or staked out, but there were still fortune hunters eager for more.

Largely because of their agitation, the government sent a force of 1,000 soldiers accompanied by newspaper reporters, map makers and a couple of geologists and minerologists to conduct a "topographical survey" of the Dakota Territory. Their leader was a young general named George Armstrong Custer.

Facing page: (top) railway siding in Nevada City, just west of Virginia City. (Bottom) reconstruction of a Victorian schoolroom, and (above) long-established citizens, Virginia City.

The survey was entirely peaceful, they said. The treaty forbidding white development of the Black Hills was sacred, they added. Custer's expedition didn't get far. The first creek they crossed, according to the minerologists, was full of gold in paying quantities.

They didn't keep their discovery to themselves, of course, and in a few days men as far away as New York were packing their knapsacks for the trip to the Dakota Territory. The American authorities, meanwhile, issued stern warnings that whites were forbidden there and dispatched Army units to keep them out. But the lure of sudden riches was too strong and little bands of prospectors managed to slip through the net and as they panned for gold they kept looking over their shoulders for Indians or soldiers.

As their numbers grew, the soldiers became frustrated and the Indians angry. It was estimated that by the spring of 1876

there were more than 11,000 gold hunters in the hills. By that point, the soldiers began to feel it was more important to protect their fellow Americans than forcefully to honor a treaty with the first Americans. It all came to a head at Little Big Horn, when General Custer came back into the picture to attack the Sioux under Sitting Bull with a force that was wiped out to the last man. It was the beginning of the end for the Indians and, less than a year later, the territory, gold and all, was declared safe for civilized men.

Among the men who took up the challenge were Fred and Moses Manuel, who wandered into a gulch not far south of Deadwood. There were 50 other miners already working there, but none had the luck of the Manuels. They uncovered

These pages: Virginia City, where wooden false fronts heighten a general store (above) and a store and saloon (facing page, top).

The romance of the Dakota goldfields is all wrapped up in the city of Deadwood, a suburb of Lead, or vice versa, depending on your point of view. Though far from abandoned, it still savors its ghosts.

Its earliest settlers were there in the days when the Army was still driving the white men out and the Sioux were on the warpath. News of the riches they had found started a mini gold rush, principally from nearby Montana, and it was at the crowded settlement of Deadwood that the soldiers decided to forget their orders.

When the first wagonloads of ore were shipped out in 1876, they passed a lone wagon headed the other way. It was a theatrical company on its way to entertain the miners. By the end of July they had built their own theater, which also doubled as a church on Sundays, a courthouse when one was needed, and a funeral parlor which was needed frequently.

Among its first customers in that role was the famous Wild Bill Hickok, who had lived in Deadwood less than a month before his untimely end. Hickok was a man who had filled just about every role available to a man in the Wild West. He had been a buffalo hunter and a soldier, a scout, a trapper and a stagecoach driver. He was also a famous gunfighter alleged to have had more than seventy-five notches on the handle of his sixgun. He used his guns in the cowtowns of Kansas, where he represented the forces of law and order. His arrival in Deadwood was very upsetting, to say the least, to the ruffians who had big plans for themselves in this new, little city. The rumor was that Hickok had been brought in by local businessmen to become Deadwood's first Marshal.

To keep that from happening the gamblers and thieves took up a collection among themselves and gave the resulting $300 to Crooked Nose Jack McCall with instructions to kill the lawman.

McCall's heart wasn't in it. Hickok's reputation as a sure shot was enough to scare the wits out of anyone. But finally, after enough whiskey, McCall tracked Hickok down. Wild Bill was at the time engaged in a friendly game of poker at the Number Ten Saloon, and fortunately his back was to the door.

One bullet to the back of the head was all it took. The cards Wild Bill was holding at the time, all black, has ever since been known as a "dead man's hand." The dead man was described by the undertaker, a man who ought to know, as "the prettiest corpse I have ever seen."

McCall, the perpetrator, was captured before he could get out of the saloon. He was tried by a jury (of his peers, of course) and found innocent.

This page: ornate touches adorn the ageing houses of Virginia City. Facing page: (top) sheriff of Virginia City. (Bottom) grave markers bear witness to the town's violent history.

a ledge of gold that proved to be the greatest such discovery in American history. It has yielded more than $500 million since they found it in 1876, and it is still producing, which explains why the town of Lead, South Dakota, just above the gulch, is not one of the ghost towns of the West.

The Manuels sold their interest in what they called "The Homestake" to a small group of California businessmen headed by George Hearst. The price was about $100,000.

Facing page: (top) a steam-era railway station, Virginia City, and (bottom and this page) a once-working steam engine and carriages, Nevada City.

Wild Bill had his share of mourners, not the least of whom was another newcomer to Deadwood, Martha Jane Canary. She was well-known all over the West as "Calamity Jane" because of an almost uncanny knack for turning up whenever anyone was in trouble. She could be counted on to nurse the sick, to comfort the dying, even to protect the rights of innocent animals. None of that is to imply that Jane was a creampuff. She left home as a very young girl for a life on the wild frontier and lived most of her days in mining camps working and carousing along with the men, most of whom swore they never knew she was a woman.

As was the case in so many of the mining camps, becoming a citizen of Deadwood seemed to require a certain amount of eccentricity. There was a woman who smoked cigars and could beat anyone in town at poker, but steadfastly refused to do so on Sundays.

There was a teamster who turned a fat profit by importing cats because he thought the dance hall girls would like them and he knew that miners would love them for their rat-catching abilities. There was a stagecoach driver who invented an iron-clad coach to protect himself and his gold shipments from highwaymen. And there were scores of highwaymen who carefully avoided coaches with circuit-riding judges aboard.

Montana hills rise beyond Virginia City's livery stables (left) and row of stores (above).

If there were mining camps that didn't have gamblers and willing women, there were none that didn't have highwaymen. And if there was a Valhalla for these desperadoes, it surely must have been Bannack, the first capital of Montana and the scene of the Territory's first gold strike.

When the gold was discovered there in 1862, prospectors moved in quickly from California and Nevada, but just as quickly it drew an unusual number of outcasts determined to get rich the easy way. One of the reasons was that justice in Bannack was in the hands of Sheriff Henry Plummer, himself a fugitive from justice hired, apparently, on the theory that it takes one to know one. But the desperadoes knew him well and together they set up headquarters, with Plummer as their leader, in Skinner's Saloon next door to the Territorial Capitol building.

Built in Tombstone (these pages) in 1881, the Bird Cage Theatre (facing page, top) remains virtually unchanged.

They infiltrated all the stage stations for miles around and knew who was on each stagecoach, how much gold dust they were carrying and whether or not there was a major shipment of gold aboard. And, of course, Plummer told them everything he knew.

After the gang had murdered close to 100 citizens, the miners formed a vigilante committee and exiled those they didn't dispatch on the spot. But it never dawned on them that the mastermind behind it all was their own sheriff. It took them two years to figure that out, even though Plummer hadn't been very careful in covering his tracks, and had even been personally involved in many of the holdups. When they did catch up with him, he and two deputies were taken out to Hangman's Gulch, where justice was finally served. His last words were, "I'm too wicked to die." He was probably right. But they hanged him anyway.

In his prime, he was so highly respected as a lawman that he was also appointed sheriff of the twin cities of Nevada City and Virginia City in Alder Gulch, about 100 miles to the east.

It was in Nevada City that the vigilante committee was first formed and their first culprit very nearly cheated them out of the pleasure of hanging him. As they were riding with him on the way back to town, he turned to one of the amateur lawmen and said, "I'll bet you $50 that my horse can outrun any horse in this posse." No man from any mining camp anywhere could have resisted a challenge like that, and this group was no exception. Before they could say "you're on!" he was off, riding as fast as he could into the hills. It took them two hours to catch up with him, but within another hour his body was swinging in the breeze.

Virginia City, which became the most important mining town in the Montana gold rush and wrested the honor of being designated the Territorial Capital from Bannack, has the same name as the famous city in Nevada, but it came by it in a much different way. Most of the miners who founded it in 1863 were strong sympathizers with the South in the Civil

War that was still raging back East. They voted to name their camp Varina, after the wife of Confederate President Jefferson Davis. The judge who was called in to make it official, on the other hand, had sympathies with the Northern cause and let them know in no uncertain terms that he wouldn't be a party to such a travesty. He finally agreed to a compromise and named the place Virginia. It probably wouldn't have mattered. None of them had a good notion of how the war was going and most didn't care even though their newspaper, *The Montana Post*, tried to keep them informed through a column of "News From America."

They were much more interested in what was going on right around home. They eagerly watched the activities of the Lyceum Committee, a group that had been formed to bring

Many of Tombstone's original buildings have been restored, and today the town (these pages) is a popular tourist attraction.

SALOON

uplift and culture to the camp in the form of touring musicians and lecturers. They were more interested in the activities of the local fire company, goings-on in saloons that they may have missed and the price of a haircut in case they should ever feel the need for one.

Their newspaper kept them up-to-date on the posturings of their local politicians, too, an important service in the Capital City. It also told them of gold strikes elsewhere, which was often a signal for miners to pick up stakes and move on. The biggest exodus took place at the beginning of 1865, and most people began predicting that Virginia City was about to become yet another ghost town. But more than a dozen years later, she was still going strong. An 1879 guide to the state said that it had become a "steady business city."

At about the time that Virginia City seemed to be drying up, the miners further west in the mountains of Idaho were still fighting off hostile Indians. In Silver City, the mines and

*These pages and overleaf: re-enactment of the gunfight at the O.K. Corral, Tombstone, Arizona.*

most of the buildings were turned into fortresses to protect its citizens from the spears and arrows of the Nez Perce braves. But, in spite of it, business was steady in the saloons, the Debating Club met regularly every Thursday and the Masons and Odd Fellows went through their rituals with the same dedication the Indians lavished on their war.

Indians or no, there was a city to be built and riches to be taken from the ground. In less than six months from the time the first miner arrived, there wasn't a tree left in sight, every one for miles around had been cut for buildings and for the sluices so important to the business at hand. In less than five years, just one of the two lodes under the city produced nearly $3 million in gold and silver.

When they weren't fighting off Indians, they sometimes fought among themselves. When an aggressive group of prospectors found a particularly rich vein and staked their claim to it, another group working nearby pointed out that it overlapped a claim they were already working on. The response was a solid fort and armed thugs at the entrance to the new mine. The whole affair wound up in court in a case that was so complicated that both litigants were forced to sell out to a third party, an Oregon syndicate.

The syndicate did well. The ore proved to be worth nearly $5,000 a ton and in ten years yielded some $4 million. The ore was so pure it won a gold medal (as if that seemed appropriate) at a Paris exposition. The company probably could have done much better, but one of its officers disappeared one day with all the funds and the status of the mine, ironically called "The Poor Man," was once again a matter for the courts to decide. The judge opted for shutting it down again and it stayed closed for the next dozen years. By the time it reopened, the action had shifted to new towns like Dewey and De Lamar a few miles down the road. All of them are just memories today. Just like the Indians they fought.

Of all the Indians who are part of America's history, one whose name stands out above most of the rest is the Apache known as Cochise. The Apaches were never what you'd call friendly, but Cochise turned hostility into a fine art after an incident with the U.S. Cavalry in 1860. The Indians had taken hostages in retaliation for the false arrest of some of their braves and the Americans refused to negotiate, demanding the immediate and unconditional return of the prisoners. Cochise responded by killing the hostages. The Americans retaliated by killing the Indians they were holding and the fat, as they say, was in the fire. The dead Indians happened to be relatives of the chief.

The bloody war that started that day lasted until Cochise died 14 years later. But even after that it took a very brave man even to think about going near the San Pedro Valley in Southeastern Arizona.

Edward Schieffelin was such a man. He was also as stubborn as he was brave. Schieffelin was convinced there were riches under those treeless hills and that he was going to find them in spite of the Apaches.

His first move was to explore the territory in the company of Cavalry patrols. It didn't give him a lot of time to dig, but at least he came back alive. By then, in 1877, the soldiers had seen prospectors all over the West and were generally convinced that they were all a little "touched in the head." But they knew they were harmless and fun to have around as the butt of their jokes. In Schieffelin's case their favorite joke

became a name on the map of Arizona and a legend in the history of the West.

"The only stone you're going to find out there," they told him, "is your tombstone." A few months later, when Ed found traces of silver in Apache country, he named his claim "Tombstone." The following year he found a better one and named it "The Graveyard." His third, a lode of silver that assayed at $15,000 a ton, he called "The Lucky Cuss." He probably didn't consider it a stroke of luck, though, because when news of his discovery leaked out he suddenly began acquiring lots of new neighbors.

In spite of the fact that Cochise's mantle had passed to the equally terrifying Geronimo, and that another Apache chief named Victorio kept whites on edge from his base across the border in Mexico, the San Pedro Valley was suddenly very attractive to white men. The idea of getting rich can do strange things to a man.

The city of Tombstone, set high on a mesa overlooking the desert, was seventy-five very rugged miles from the county seat at Tucson, and the trip to or from the territorial capital at Prescott took more than a week. The Apaches made either trip just about unthinkable, so Tombstone was established without any links to any formal sort of law enforcement or, it should be added, official interference. Considering that the men who settled there in general fit classic textbook definitions of "rugged individualism," it's no wonder that Tombstone, Arizona, is often considered one of the wildest towns the West has ever produced.

Strangely, it was a relatively civilized place in its first years. The miners who had staked claims before there was a city were at violent odds with businessmen who bought the same land later, but almost nobody was there for any reason except to get rich and there was plenty to go around. The trouble started when they became an official entity in the Territory of Arizona, and then had the advantages of law enforcement and the justice system provided by the courts. Being "official" made Tombstone a mecca for lawyers and other professional people. The new status lured politicians with a lust for patronage, and it brought in businessmen who went beyond the handful of saloons and hardware stores, livery stables and rooming houses that served the mining camp, but were obviously not adequate to serve a city that had become a county seat.

Facing page: oil lamps and Victorian advertising above a shaded boardwalk, Tombstone.

By 1881, Ed Schieffelin had 6,000 neighbors in Tombstone. The population eventually went as high as 20,000. There may have been a lot more if the six shooter had never been invented.

Among the great practitioners of the art of being quick on the draw and shooting before being shot was the combination lawman/gambler Wyatt Earp, the Deputy U.S. Marshal in Tombstone. Wyatt and his brothers had all made big names for themselves as lawmen back in the cowtowns of Kansas, as had their friend Bat Masterson who went to Tombstone with them. Since there was relatively little money in keeping the peace, they all augmented their income by gambling and obviously there was no better place than Tombstone for them to make their home.

Though poker was the game of choice in most of the Western mining camps, the choice of professionals like Masterson and the Earps was usually faro. It was a simple game that took its name from the fact that the cards used to play had pictures of an Egyptian pharaoh printed on the back. The cards were dealt mechanically from a closed box two at a time and placed on a printed board. Participants bet on each deal whether the cards would match the next space on the board. If the two cards dealt were the same, the house split the winnings. It was a simple game with lots of action and, because of the fact that the cards were untouched by human hands, it would seem relatively safe from the possibility of cheating. But American ingenuity being what it is, almost no one got into a game without a trusty Smith and Wesson or Colt revolver handy.

If there was money to be made with a faro box or in a mine shaft, Tombstone offered an alternative many of the mining boom towns didn't have. Before the boom, there was no railroad anywhere in the Arizona Territory, but by 1881 the Southern Pacific had moved east to Tucson. Within a year or two it had linked up with the Santa Fe and for the first time it was possible to ship cattle anywhere in the country. The grasslands in the southeastern corner of Arizona were lush and Tombstone itself constituted a rich market close by. It all added up to an opportunity no cattle baron could resist. And where there are cattlemen, you can be sure there are also cattle rustlers. Both breeds did very well in Tombstone.

Opportunities for bad guys in the West had largely dried up by the late 1880s, but the Arizona climate gave them a chance at a few more good years. Along with the rustlers and horse thieves came highwaymen and other assorted fugitives from justice, including the remnants of the old Sam Bass gang and men who had learned their trade from Jesse and Frank James. The idea of organized outlaw gangs had long since proven itself in the West, but in Tombstone territory the idea flourished because of the incredible collection of seasoned outlaws lured there by the promise of

At the height of its importance as a gold and silver mining town in the early 1880s, Tombstone (these pages) is still very much alive, the old co-existing with the new.

easy pickings at a point in their careers where expanding population had made their trade more dangerous and less profitable elsewhere. The Arizona Territory was their last frontier.

At first they operated from isolated ranches, stealing livestock, holding up stagecoaches and generally instituting a reign of terror that sometimes made the Apaches seem like

This page: period costume strengthens the illusion that Tombstone's past still lives. Facing page: bleak memorials to the dead on Boot Hill.

good neighbors. But it was only a matter of time before they began to get bold enough to come out of hiding. By then they felt they were ready to take over the whole town of Tombstone. They began making their presence felt with open daylight raids. In a single, ten-day period, rustlers gunned down 14 innocent Tombstone citizens. Then they realized they didn't have to go to all that trouble. They were well-organized enough to use more subtle methods. And they were rich enough to buy any political officials who might be for sale.

Many were, but it isn't easy to know who among Tombstone's leaders were honest and who were not. There was, on the other hand, a powerful "Law and Order League," and one of its more prominent members was Wyatt Earp. His best friend, the former dentist Doc Holliday, was also a member, though. Holliday was well-known for his activities on the other side of the law and was, in fact, wanted in several places for murder. Earp himself remembered Holliday as "the most skilful gambler and the nerviest,

speediest, deadliest man with a sixgun I ever knew." Earp also remembered a man who "could punish an enormous amount of whiskey." He said that "two or three quarts of whiskey a day was not unusual for Doc." But he added that the man never got drunk even though it often took a pint of whiskey to get him started in the morning.

But, of course, drinking and gambling and drawing a gun didn't make a man seem evil in the glory days of the West, and no one thought it the least bit unusual that such a man would be a stalwart in the Law and Order League.

Wyatt Earp and Doc Holliday were key figures in what has often been called the greatest gunfight the West has even seen.

By mid-1881, Wyatt's brother Virgil had become the City Marshal of Tombstone and along with the job he took on a host of special enemies, including the Clanton and McLowry brothers, who let it be known that they not only hated Virgil, but the same went for his brothers Wyatt and Morgan.

It all came to a head on the afternoon of October 26 in front of the O.K. Corral. That morning Frank and Tom McLowry and Ike and Billy Clanton had appeared in town with guns and let it be known that they were going to reduce the population of Tombstone a little. The Earps decided to take the initiative and, with Doc Holliday at their side, took an after-lunch stroll. It should be mentioned that all four were lean and tough six-footers and for this occasion all were dressed from head to foot in black. Holliday wore an overcoat which concealed a shotgun. The other three wore their guns at their side. It was a sight that might have turned away just about any kind of wrath. In this case it didn't.

When Virgil ordered them to drop their guns, the outlaws fired them instead, not at Virgil, mind you, but at his brother Wyatt. The bullets missed their mark and, before they could shoot again, Wyatt put a bullet into Frank McLowry's stomach and Holliday fired the shotgun at his brother, Tom. Frank was killed outright. Tom McLowry turned and ran but died before he could reach the corner. Young Billy Clanton, meanwhile, opened fire on the Earps but took three bullets in return. Ike Clanton escaped, but was stopped by the crowd of spectators and taken to jail. Virgil and Morgan Earp were both wounded, though neither seriously. And Wyatt Earp, the principal target, as well as his buddy Doc Holliday, escaped without so much as a scratch.

These pages and overleaf: the color and competition of the now less deadly gunfight revived in Tombstone.

The next morning, one local newspaper reported that: "The feeling of the better class of citizens is that the Marshal and his posse acted solely in the right in attempting to disarm the cowboys and that it was a case of kill or be killed."

But was it? No one knows for sure what really happened on that October afternoon. As soon as the shooting stopped, a

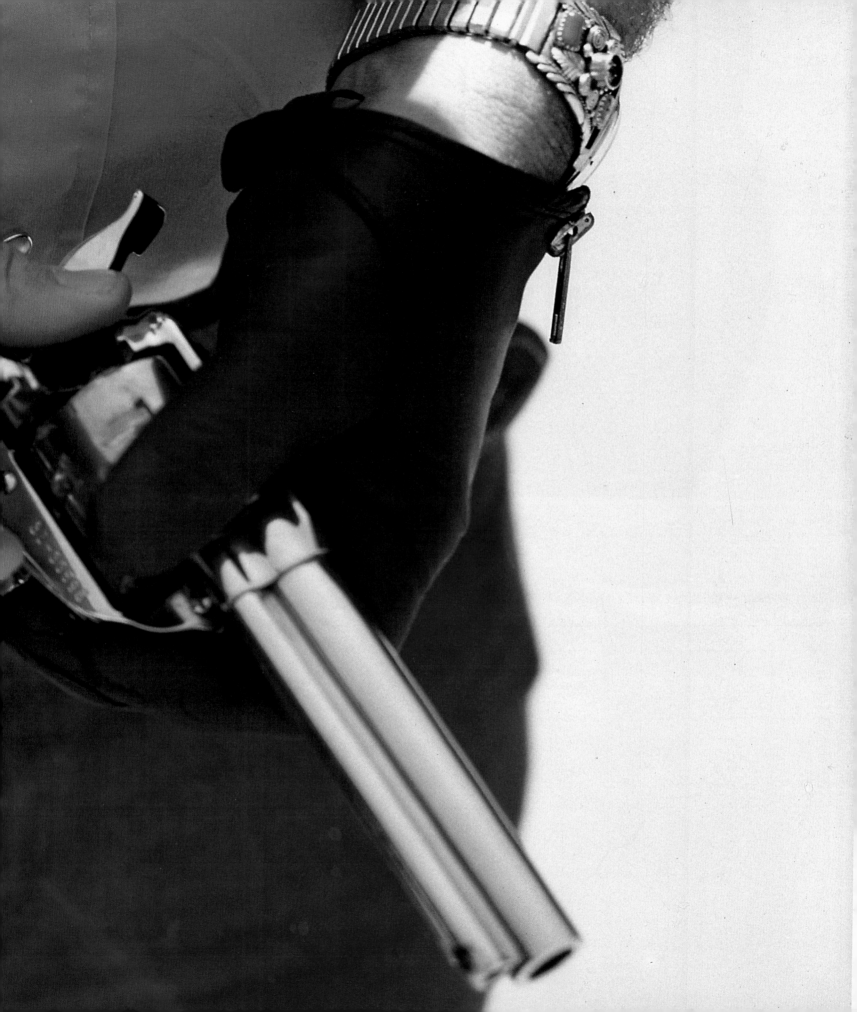

These pages: cowboys and lawmen meet to contest the speed of the draw, Tombstone. Overleaf: the old west restored and reproduced.

huge delegation of Tombstone's citizens, "better class" and otherwise, went over to the O.K. Corral to have a look around. In the process, they destroyed all of the evidence that might have been used to reconstruct the sequence of events. There had been spectators, but none foolish enough to have been close enough to be called eyewitnesses. The sheriff himself was too busy to conduct an immediate investigation. He was trying to arrest Wyatt Earp.

According to the sheriff, the Clantons and McLowrys were not armed. He had taken their guns himself, he said, and added that he had told the Earps what he had done before the fight started. Wyatt refused to go to jail, of course, and the crowd agreed with him. It was decided that the Earps would be put in the custody of a vigilante committee who set up a 24-hour guard, not to keep them prisoner, but to protect them from reprisals.

The next morning, in addition to the newspaper report that washed away their possible sins, there were other reports that said the Earps were guilty of "wanton murder." The sheriff's story that the "cowboys" were all unarmed was altered to one that had just two of them defenseless but the cowboy partisans swore that when the Earp party rounded the corner they raised their hands in surrender and that the two armed men never fired until fired upon.

It was the prime topic of conversation in Tombstone for months. One of the dead men, Billy Clanton, would have been pleased by some of the things they were saying about

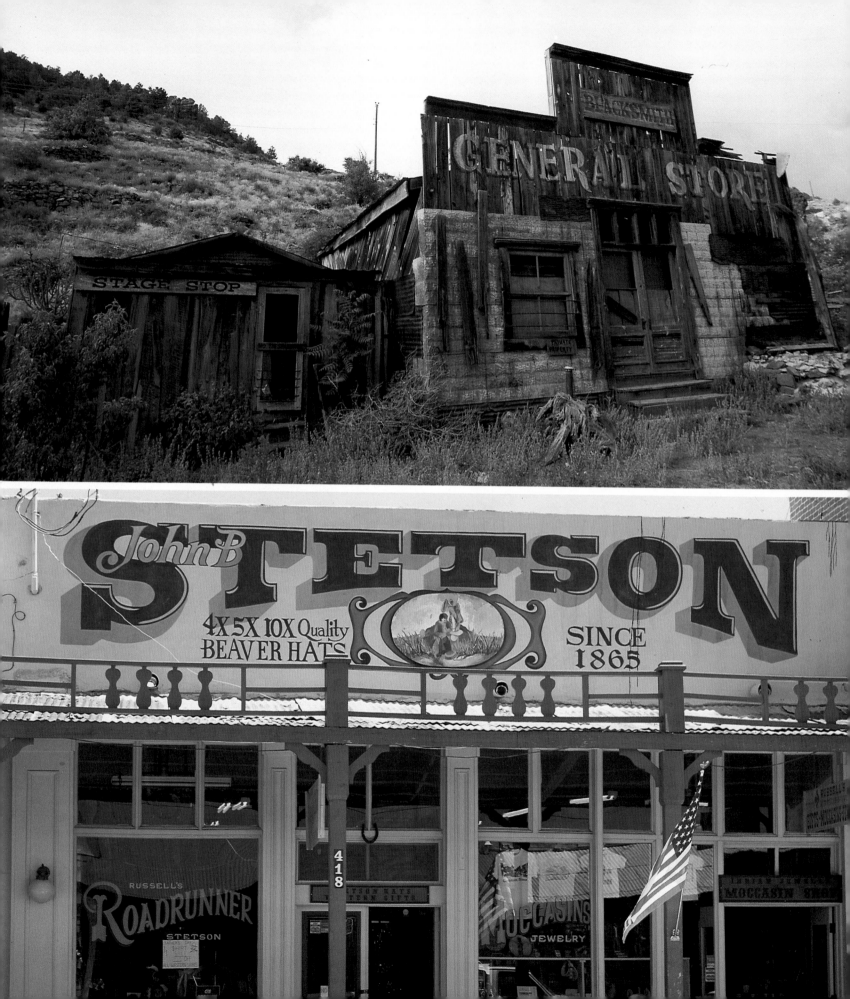

Facing page: (top) the neglected, and (bottom) the refurbished face of Tombstone (this page).

him. He was just a boy, they said, not more than fifteen or so (he was really just short of twenty). It was true, they said, that he had been a desperado as a youngster, a sort of juvenile delinquent, but he had made a promise to his dying mother that he would be a good boy. Part of the promise was that he wouldn't die with his boots on and, in fact, they said, when he knew he was dying, his last desperate plea was to have his boots removed.

The story continued that Billy's brother Ike might have escaped with his life if he hadn't run toward Wyatt, unarmed of course, in a brave but futile attempt to save the lad's life.

His pleas fell on deaf ears, according to the story, and poor Billy was cut down before he ever had a chance to reach his prime.

The Earps were eventually acquitted in court, but the affair divided Tombstone until Tombstone itself eventually died. Wyatt wandered from one boom town to another for the rest of his life. By the time he died in Los Angeles in 1929, he was a wealthy man. Doc Holliday died in Colorado three years after the shootout, without his boots on.

People who lived in almost any of the mining metropolises usually knew that their city would eventually die, and it wasn't at all uncommon for many of them to have lived in several different ones. But if the end was predictable for Tombstone, almost no one connected with it in its early days could have guessed the cause of death.

Who could have known that this city overlooking the Arizona desert would drown?

By the beginning of 1886, less than ten years after Ed Schieffelin arrived there, the mines began to show signs of running out of silver. The answer to that was to dig deeper, but when the depth reached 500 feet they struck water. Pumps were installed, but two of the biggest were each destroyed by fires. By the end of the decade, Tombstone was a ghost town. There have been several attempts to revive it in the years since, but the cost of removing all that water (they were pumping out a steady 8 million gallons a day in 1901) has driven every company that tried it into bankruptcy.

The idea of modern machinery and corporate giants fighting off bankruptcy doesn't quite square with the image the words "ghost town" conjures up. Yet some of the towns in the West that are shadows of their former selves were booming when your grandfather was a boy. One such town was Cripple Creek, Colorado. It was incorporated during the silver panic that wiped out Haw Tabor in 1893. Within a year its population reached as high as 20,000 because, when the Government stopped buying silver, gold became the metal of choice and the gold in Cripple Creek was both plentiful and easy to find. In fact, it produced nearly $450 million worth of gold in the early years of the 20th century, a record matched only by the Homestake in South Dakota.

Cripple Creek was a modern metropolis whose population was well over 50,000 by 1910. Its streets were lit with electric lights and folks got from one end of town to the other in a newfangled electric streetcar. Its restaurants and hotels catered to the most cosmopolitan of tastes and the entertainment available rivaled anything on the stages of New York or Boston. Among the attractions were the Marx Brothers, who never forgot the place because the Vaudeville troupe that took them there disbanded at Cripple Creek, leaving them high and dry. Groucho was forced to take a job as a delivery boy to raise the cash to get himself and his brothers down out of the mountains.

They had their choice of three different railroads. A fellow passenger might have been the future speakeasy queen, Texas Guinan, tired of her job as a church organist and on her way to the big time back East. They might also have rubbed shoulders with the future heavyweight boxing champion Jack Dempsey, a Cripple Creek miner who fought his first fight in the opera house there and left town with his $50 purse. All of them might also have noticed a young Lowell Thomas standing on the station platform and thinking of the faraway places that would make him one of the first journalists to become famous as a radio broadcaster.

But for all its links with our generation, the thing that will make Cripple Creek, Colorado known to future generations is its part in the history of organized labor in America.

The first labor union in the United States was the Knights of Labor, which made its presence known by a job action in Leadville in the 1870s. Haw Tabor and his Highland Guards ran them out of town for having the effrontery to ask for a raise to $3.75 for each 10-hour day, and the straight $3 wage held firm.

The union was effectively broken but the idea kept simmering until 1892, when the newly-formed Western Federation of Miners staged an unsuccessful strike in Coeur D'Alene, Idaho. They regrouped in Butte, Montana and swore to each other that they would never "lose" another strike. They had their chance to test their strength in Cripple Creek in 1894.

Because of a depression back East, Cripple Creek had a huge surplus of labor in the form of out-of-work men who had gone to the gold fields pleased to swing a pick for 10 hours for $3. But the new union wanted more for its members and was well-enough organized to have set up a benefit program for men willing to participate in their general strike.

The first strike lasted five months, during which time the mine owners brought in tough replacements, with the result that the governor called in the militia. It was settled when the owners reduced the workday to eight hours, but didn't raise the salary. Not all the workers agreed with the settlement, though, and the owners were forced to hire their own "deputies," brawlers from all over the West. The first trainload of them was turned around by angry miners in a fight that cost the lives of two of them. A few days later an ore car loaded with dynamite was sent crashing into a mine shaft occupied by a few of the strike-breakers who had slipped into the territory. No one was killed, but the mine was destroyed and both sides, weary of violence, came to a shaky agreement.

Though the strike didn't advance the cause of the miners a whole lot, the union that represented them came away stronger than ever, and all America began getting the message that trade unionism was an idea both workers and management were going to have to begin taking seriously.

There were dozens of strikes in mining camps all over the West after that and, even though they lost many of them, the Western Federation of Miners learned from each of them. By 1903, they were ready to put the things they learned to the acid test and the battleground, once again, was Cripple Creek.

Facing page: Tombstone's latterday "cowboys."

By then their membership west of the Rockies had grown to more than 200,000 and in towns like Cripple Creek the W.F.M. was powerful enough to control not only the miners but the local government as well. And by 1903, the W.F.M. had dedicated itself to something more than higher wages, shorter hours and better working conditions. Their case had turned to "... a change in social and economic conditions that will result in a complete revolution of the present system of industrial slavery." Their enemies called them Bolsheviks.

The Cripple Creek strike dragged on uneventfully for a month or two until the owners hired armed guards and reopened some of the mines with non-union workers. The workers retaliated by carrying guns on their picket lines and beating up anyone who tried to cross them. The governor retaliated further by calling out the militia again and the battle lines were drawn.

These page: Tombstone, where, each October, the people recreate their town's 1880s era in the three-day celebrations of "Helldorado Days".

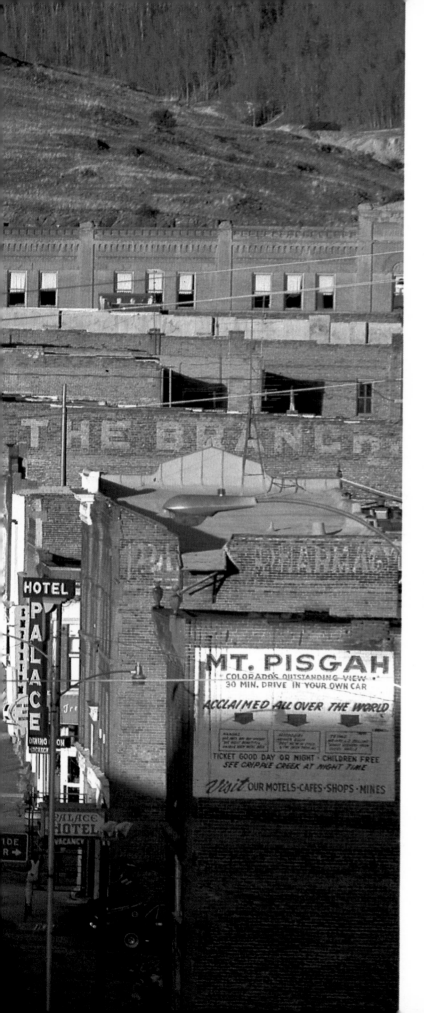

Cripple Creek became an armed camp, with troops patrolling the streets with fixed bayonets and public buildings protected by Gatling guns. The show of force allowed the mines to reopen using strikebreakers and the battle seethed under the surface for five months. It came to a head when a union official managed to make his way into the depths of one of the district's biggest mines which he destroyed with a charge of dynamite, in the process killing both the superintendant and the foreman.

Previous pages: (insets) abandoned buildings lie scattered across the landscape (main picture) around Cripple Creek, Colorado. Left: red-brick buildings in Cripple Creek (above).

That action resulted in strict new laws that included a tight curfew and the threat of arrest for any able-bodied man who didn't seem to have a job. Any sort of union activity was outlawed under threat of deportation.

The laws seemed to work. The mines were humming again, the so-called radicals were either penned up in a stockade or long-since run out of town and it seemed safe to walk the streets of Cripple Creek again. The troops were withdrawn in June, 1904. But the authorities had underestimated the W.F.M. On June 6 the railroad station was destroyed in a bomb blast that killed 15 men and wounded dozens of others. The next day the troops were back rounding up the usual suspects. Anyone who had even remote sympathy with the union was loaded into a train with a one-way ticket to the state line and a strong warning never to come back to Colorado again, not even for a weekend of skiing.

Every mine was shut while the authorities searched for union sympathizers. They eventually deported some 250 of them, and even more slipped away before they could be caught in the net.

Above: a rusting vehicle, and (facing page, top) a deserted homestead, in Cripple Creek. Facing page: (bottom) gravestone of the celebrated hostess of a high-class Cripple Creek brothel.

Things went back to normal after that, the union was broken and was never able to operate seriously in the West again. Its more zealous organizers went east to found the Industrial Workers of the World. Cripple Creek itself began to grow again and reached the height of its opulence in 1908. By then they had not only wiped out the stigma of labor unrest, but the city had been completely rebuilt after two disastrous fires destroyed every building in 1906. The new city boasted wide streets and tall buildings (as high as four stories!) built

PEARL DE VERE
DIED
JUNE 5, 1897

Though many of the original structures of Cripple Creek (these pages) were destroyed by fire in 1905, some early buildings survive and remain in use, giving charm and atmosphere to this historic Colorado gold town.

entirely of brick. Some were so elegant they were moved to nearby Colorado Springs when the boom ended. It ended at the same time the rest of the world was beginning to worry about the oncoming war in Europe and the real Bolsheviks were plotting the overthrow of Russia's Czar.

By the early years of the 20th century the great rushes westward in search of gold and silver had become a romantic part of past history, whose legacy is often not much more than hard-to-find, tumble-down ghost towns. But are there real ghosts out there?
Some people say there are.

If there are such things, one of the more likely candidates would be Ed Ennis, who believed very strongly in the possibility. Ed was a New Yorker who decided to use a little science to get rich in the Colorado mountains. The science he chose was spiritualism. He gave most of his life's savings to a medium who said that the talk of the ethereal world was a lake of pure silver under the San Juan Mountains near the Continental Divide. He got a lot more than talk for his money. The medium not only told him exactly where the silver lake was, but how to dig a shaft to get at it.

Ed packed his bags and within a month had started digging the shaft, at the same time building a fancy mansion nearby; he was that sure he was about to become a wealthy man. His shaft hadn't gone far when he did, indeed, find silver good enough to yield up to $7,500 a ton. It would have made any prospector deliriously happy, but Ed Ennis's mentor hadn't said anything about silver that close to the surface so he

Above: the Rocky Mountains, beyond the hills around Cripple Creek (facing page). The town grew up following the discovery of one of the world's largest gold fields in about 1891. At the height of productivity, in 1901, it yielded almost $25 million.

packed up and went back to New York for another seance. When he got back the following spring, he told his workers to begin digging in another direction. Almost daily he changed the direction of his shaft, often striking silver, but not finding a lake of it. He had made an arrangement to communicate with the medium through dreams, and possibly because of the great distance between New York and Colorado, the message wasn't always clear.

He kept snaking through the belly of the mountain until his money ran out, and finally he was forced to sell his claims. The new owners, working without the benefit of the science